by Claire Daniel
illustrated by Nicole Tadgell

SCHOOL PUBLISHERS

Copyright © by Harcourt, Inc.

All rights reserved. No part of this publication may be reproduced or transmitted in any form or by any means, electronic or mechanical, including photocopy, recording, or any information storage and retrieval system, without permission in writing from the publisher.

Requests for permission to make copies of any part of the work should be addressed to School Permissions and Copyrights, Harcourt, Inc., 6277 Sea Harbor Drive, Orlando, Florida 32887–6777. Fax: 407-345-2418.

HARCOURT and the Harcourt Logo are trademarks of Harcourt, Inc., registered in the United States of America and/or other jurisdictions.

Printed in Mexico

ISBN 10: 0-15-350271-1
ISBN 13: 978-0-15-350271-2

Ordering Options
ISBN 10: 0-15-349940-0 (Grade 5 ELL Collection)
ISBN 13: 978-0-15-349940-1 (Grade 5 ELL Collection)
ISBN 10: 0-15-357305-8 (package of 5)
ISBN 13: 978-0-15-357305-7 (package of 5)

If you have received these materials as examination copies free of charge, Harcourt School Publishers retains title to the materials and they may not be resold. Resale of examination copies is strictly prohibited and is illegal.

Possession of this publication in print format does not entitle users to convert this publication, or any portion of it, into electronic format.

2 3 4 5 6 7 8 9 10   126   12 11 10 09 08 07

You have been moving since the day you were born. You were always moving your hands, arms, fingers, and toes. Moving your body is an important part of your life. You must move to walk or eat your lunch. You move to play a game or climb into bed.

Moving makes your body strong and healthy. Exercise helps your body stay a healthy weight. Getting exercise is one of the most important things you can do for your body.

Your body is amazing. It can do so many things! Your body moves so well because it has bones, muscles, and joints.

Bones

Bones hold your body together. They help you move. Your body would be like jelly without bones. You would not be able to move at all!

The bones in your spine hold your body up straight. The bones in your arms, hands, and fingers help you to hold this book. The bones in your legs and hips help you to run and jump.

Bones need dairy products and dark, leafy green vegetables. Another thing that healthy bones need is exercise. Bones need to move to grow and stay strong!

Joints

Bones meet at the joints. If you feel your elbow right now, you'll find the elbow joint where your arm bends. You also have a knee joint in your leg. These joints help you move your arms and legs. Exercise keeps all your joints healthy.

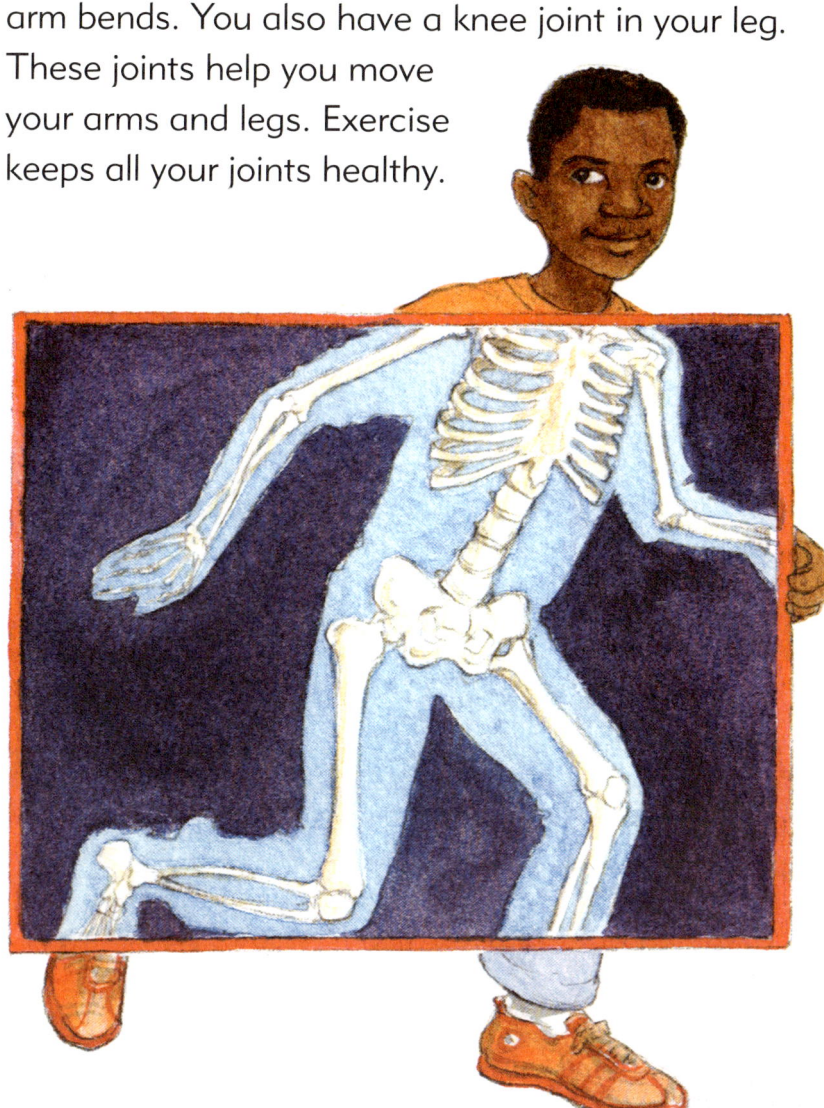

Muscles

Muscles are attached to your bones. Muscles make it possible for the bones to move. The muscles are made of groups of cells that are fibers. These fibers work together to bend or straighten different parts of your body. The brain tells the muscles what to do and where to move.

Exercise makes your muscles strong. Strong muscles make a body healthy. Be careful, though! You need to stretch your muscles during any exercise. Stretching warms up the muscles and prevents injury.

Lungs

Your muscles need oxygen to move. You bring oxygen into your lungs when you breathe. Lungs are soft organs inside your chest. Your lungs get bigger when you inhale, or take in air. Oxygen from the air travels through your lungs and into your blood. Your heart pumps the blood that is rich in oxygen through your body.

Exercise brings lots of oxygen to every part of your body. Exercise makes your lungs healthy. It makes your body strong.

Heart

Your heart is a big muscle. The heart pumps blood to all parts of your body. Your body needs more oxygen when you move. Blood comes from the lungs and enters the heart. The heart pumps the blood everywhere in your body. Your heart muscle works harder to pump the blood to the muscles when you exercise.

You help your heart to become stronger when you do aerobic exercise. *Aerobic* means "with air." Aerobic exercise means moving around to bring air to your heart and lungs. Aerobic exercise makes your heart very happy!

What is the Best Exercise?

The best exercise you can do is what you enjoy. Everyone is different, so everyone enjoys different kinds of exercise.

Aerobic Exercises

Good aerobic exercises are activities like swimming, basketball, jogging, walking quickly, soccer, or biking. Skipping, jumping rope, and hopscotch could be aerobic exercises, too!

Pay attention to your body when you run and play. Is your heart beating really fast? If so, you are doing an aerobic exercise!

Exercise Gives You Strength

Some exercises make your muscles stronger. Climbing a rope strengthens your arm and leg muscles. Doing push-ups or swinging across the monkey bars at the playground also makes your arms stronger. Just remember to be careful. Don't push yourself too hard too quickly. Other great exercises that build strong muscles are pull-ups, tug-of-war, rowing, running, skating, and riding a bike.

Muscle Flexibility

If you can bend and stretch your muscles easily without pain or muscle tightness, then you are flexible. Being flexible helps protect your body from injury when you exercise. You can become more flexible by stretching your muscles.

Can you bend over and touch your toes? You are probably flexible if you can! If you can't touch your toes, practice every day. Your body will become more flexible. Soon you will be able to touch your toes, too.

Team Sports

Some people enjoy team sports like baseball, kickball, soccer, and basketball. These sports are great aerobic exercise. They also help you learn how to work with a team.

Playing team sports can help to give you more confidence. Learning how to catch a baseball or put a basketball in a hoop feels good. Team sports help you feel better about yourself.

Team sports also help you have better coordination. This helps you make your muscles do what you want them to do. Your muscles can learn how to move in a certain way. For example, your body learns how much muscle power to use to kick a soccer ball into a goal.

Find an Exercise You Love

Not everyone likes team sports. That's okay! You can do many sports on your own. Karate is something you can do on your own. You can also become a swimmer, play tennis, or ride a bicycle. Whatever exercise you choose, you need to do it regularly. That's why it is really important to choose an exercise that you like to do.

Exercise builds a strong body. A strong body can move around and do all the things you want it to do. You will also sleep better if you exercise. You will be better able to handle stress. You feel stress when things upset you during the day like missing a bus or studying for a test.

Children who exercise often grow up to be healthier adults. Make an effort to exercise every day. Your body will thank you one day!

Scaffolded Language Development

USING -ING Point out the following sentences in the text:

> Moving makes your body strong and healthy. *(page 3)*
> Stretching warms up the muscles and prevents injury. *(page 6)*

Ask students what the sentences have in common. Confirm that each of the sentences begins with a noun that ends with *–ing*. Remind students that these words are called gerunds. Gerunds are made by adding the *–ing* ending to some verbs. Remind students that sometimes a spelling change is required when adding the *–ing* ending to a verb. Ask students to turn the following verbs into gerunds:

climb	kick	play
hit	learn	run
hop	swim	jump

🍎 Health

Exercise Poster Have students make an exercise poster by drawing a picture of some kind of exercise and writing under the picture how people can benefit from doing that exercise. Have them think of a title for their poster.

School-Home Connection

Stay in Shape Have students discuss with family members the benefits of exercise. Have them talk about exercises they could do together.

Word Count: 981